Let's All Sing …
Songs from Disney's
HIGH SCHOOL MUSICAL

SONGS FROM DISNEY'S
HIGH SCHOOL MUSICAL

COLLECTION FOR YOUNG VOICES

Arranged by Tom Anderson and John Higgins

TABLE OF CONTENTS

ISBN 978-1-4234-5585-1

Walt Disney Music Company

DISTRIBUTED BY

HAL•LEONARD®
CORPORATION
7777 W. BLUEMOUND RD. P.O. BOX 13819 MILWAUKEE, WI 53213

Visit Hal Leonard Online at
www.halleonard.com

BOP TO THE TOP

Words and Music by RANDY PETERSEN
and KEVIN QUINN
Arranged by TOM ANDERSON

BREAKING FREE

Words and Music by JAMIE HOUSTON
Arranged by TOM ANDERSON

GET'CHA HEAD IN THE GAME

Words and Music by RAY CHAM,
GREG CHAM and ANDREW SEELEY
Arranged by TOM ANDERSON

Start of Something New

Words and Music by MATTHEW GERRARD
and ROBBIE NEVIL
Arranged by TOM ANDERSON

WE'RE ALL IN THIS TOGETHER

Words and Music by MATTHEW GERRARD
and ROBBIE NEVIL
Arranged by JOHN HIGGINS

Hal Leonard proudly presents
HIGH SCHOOL MUSICAL
collections arranged specifically for young voices

LET'S ALL SING ... SONGS FROM DISNEY'S HIGH SCHOOL MUSICAL

Arranged by Tom Anderson and John Higgins

Let's all sing, just for the fun of it! Sing-along with five of your favorite songs from Disney's smash hit movie "High School Musical" in this collection that is perfect for group singing in the classroom, community or anywhere kids get together! The songs have been carefully arranged in kid-friendly ranges for unison voices with optional harmonies. The PVG includes complete piano/vocal arrangements, and the Singer Edition offers the vocal parts. Singers of all ages will love singing along with the *hot* full performance tracks on the CD recording, or use the professionally-produced accompaniment tracks for that special moment in the spotlight!

Songs include: *Bop to the Top, Breaking Free, Get'cha Head in the Game, Start of Something New, We're All in This Together.*

09971141	Piano/Vocal/Guitar	$14.95
09971142	Singer Edition	$ 2.95
09971143	Singer Edition 10-Pak	$24.95
09971144	Performance/Accompaniment CD	$45.00

LET'S ALL SING ... SONGS FROM DISNEY'S HIGH SCHOOL MUSICAL 2

Arranged by Tom Anderson

The HSM gang is back together … for more singing, dancing and a summer of fun in the sun! Kids of all ages will enjoy singing these 5 favorite songs from Disney's popular *High School Musical 2*! Easy-to-sing arrangements for unison singing with some optional harmonies are sure to hit the mark for group singing in the classroom, community or on stage! Fully accompanied songs are featured in the PVG, and the handy Singer Edition offers vocal parts only. Sing-along with the *hot* performance tracks on the CD recording, or perform with the professionally-orchestrated accompaniment tracks for your *fun in the sun*!

Songs include: *All for One, Fabulous, Gotta Go My Own Way, What Time Is It, You Are the Music in Me.*

09971145	Piano/Vocal/Guitar	$14.95
09971146	Singer Edition	$ 2.95
09971147	Singer Edition 10-Pak	$24.95
09971148	Performance/Accompaniment CD	$45.00